A Midsummer's Journey
with the Sidhe

David Spangler

art by Jeremy Berg

Midsummer's day, June 21

On a pleasant Midsummer's Day in the month of June, I decided to celebrate the longest day of the year by hiking in the hills near where I live. There I came upon an old and weather-beaten stone that looked as if it had lain there in the ground forever. Feeling tired, I sat upon this stone to rest a moment. As I did so, it was as if a deep peace enfolded me. I felt as if the stone were some ancient ancestor with roots not only deep in the earth but deep in time as well. I felt in touch with beginnings and with the origins of things.

As I sat there, contemplating this strange feeling, I began to feel drowsy. My eyelids grew heavy and I could feel my head nodding. The sense of peacefulness grew even deeper. I knew I was about to slumber on this warm stone, and I felt willing to go with it, to sink into a pleasant and refreshing sleep.

But then it was as if I heard a voice. "Open your eyes and see!" I was startled from my drowsiness. I raised my head, my eyes now wide open. To my astonishment, rising behind me was a hill that I would have sworn had not been there before. How could I have missed it? As I sprang to my feet in wonder, I realized that this was no ordinary hill, but a Howe, a hollow hill carved out who knew how long ago by some long-forgotten ancient people. Was it an ancient tomb or a temple? I had no idea. But then I saw that there was an opening into the hill and a path leading to it. And were those stars I saw within? Stars inside the earth?

Being an adventurous sort, I decided to enter the hill and see what wonders it might hold, but before I could set my feet on the path leading into it, I heard the voice again, deep and resonant in my mind. "Look around," it said once more. I whirled about, but I could see no one nearby. It felt as if the voice came from the land itself. "Before you enter, walk the circle," it said.

What circle?

But then as if by magic—and surely I was in the presence of a strange and wondrous magic—I saw a standing stone at the beginning of the path, no more than two yards south from the opening into the hollow hill. Where it had come from, I had no idea. The peacefulness I had felt while reclining on the ancestor stone remained with me. Perhaps, I thought, I am really only dreaming, though everything felt very solid and real to me.

I went over to the standing stone, noting that from one angle it resembled an old bearded man dressed in a robe that reached to his feet. It made me think of a wizard, and something in me responded affirmatively, saying, "Yes, this is the Wizard's Stone." As I stood near it, it seemed filled with the power to make things happen.

Sure enough, I saw another stone standing not far away but to the east of the Howe. Remembering the request to "walk the circle," I made my way over to it. It was a tall and mighty stone, and it seemed to me to command the approach from the east. Touching it, I thought I heard the word "Guardian" in my mind, and then, "I hold and protect the boundaries." Indeed, standing next to it, I felt a curious sensation of safety and well-being.

I continued my walk around the Howe, this time going to the north. Here was a standing stone whose gentle curves gave me a sense of a feminine presence. This was heightened by moss growing down one side of it, like a fall of green hair. I wondered what this stone might be, and the voice in my head, now growing familiar if no less strange, said, "I am the Bard. I know the pathways and the directions, the stories and the songs so you can navigate under the stars." And as I stood there, I felt myself in the presence of knowledge and wisdom.

This time I pressed on to the west, traveling counter-clockwise around the Howe. The light from the late afternoon sun caught a fourth standing stone at an angle, making it appear in shadow, a tall presence that was slightly menacing. What might this one be? I wondered. Beyond it was a river, which I had not known was present in these hills. Mystery upon mystery! This time the mysterious voice said, "I am the Reaper," and when I heard it, I could not help but shiver. But then the voice went on in a more reassuring tone. "I am the harvest and I lead not to endings but new beginnings. Fear me not!"

This was all well and good, and I took these reassuring words to heart, but still, I admit I was glad to continue on my way around the Howe, now ending up once more at the Wizard stone that stood in the south before the path that led to the Howe's entrance. "All right," I said out loud to my invisible companion. "I have walked the circle. May I now enter the hill before me?"

"Not yet," came the words, whispering in my mind. "You have met my Guardians, but there are others still to know. There is a wider circle which you must walk. Look!"

I looked to the south, and beyond the Wizard stone, three new stones appeared, one atop the other two, all together forming a portal. Where had they come from? This was magical indeed.

I walked up to this portal and placed my hand upon one of the stones. "And who are you?" I asked. No answer. So I stepped through, and immediately it was as though I felt the land around me as a presence, as if I stepped not upon the rich earth but into it. "I am the Gate of Earth and of the Light within it," came the familiar voice.

I stepped back through the Portal, and felt the presence of the land recede, though it did not disappear. The mysterious words continued. "Through this gate come the forces of the land, the spirit of the Earth, to meet the forces of the Stars and the spirit of the Cosmos." I looked about but saw no stars, only the blue of the sky, fleeced with clouds. I looked north towards the Howe and the path leading into it. It seemed odd to me that this path proceeded from the portal to the south and not from the east which is so traditionally the place of beginnings. But then I remembered the plants who begin their life as seeds deep within the earth, and I thought, life begins even before the sun rises to see it.

Thinking of the sun, I looked to the east. There I saw a new standing stone, one covered with markings. I walked towards it, and as I did, a falcon flew by overhead, landing on the stone where it spread its wings before me as if in greeting—or in warning. When I came close, I saw carvings on the side of the stone. This time the voice said, "I am the stone of Partnership, of Spirit partnering form, of form partnering Spirit, giving birth to what is possible and to what seeks birth. "

Continuing on, I saw ahead of me further to the east another portal, three more stones with one upon the other two. A seagull flew above it. Coming up to it, I looked through and was astonished to see the rising sun, even though I knew it was late afternoon. What magic was this? The voice of my invisible companion said, "This is the Gate of Dawn. This is the portal of manifestation, the portal of boundaries." I stepped through, and I was in a new day, the sun just rising, and all around me I felt a spirit of potentials taking form. I stepped back, and I was once again where the late afternoon sun was plunging towards the western horizon.

Remembering that I needed to walk the circle, I continued on, this time towards the north, where I saw yet another standing stone and beyond it in the distance another portal.

I walked to the stone. Like the Stone of Partnership to the south of me, this one too had a strange carving upon it, a diamond with a circle within it. While pondering its meaning, the voice whispered to me, "This shows the four corners of the world and the soul within it. This is the Stone of Direction. It maps the world and helps you find your way."

Knowing I was truly in a magical place, I felt maps and directions would be a good thing so I would not lose my way. I placed my hand upon the stone hoping for some realizations, but all I felt was the need to continue. So I walked on to the next portal I had seen.

Unlike the first two, this one had three stones on the bottom and a fourth on top. Did this have some special meaning? I didn't know. Perhaps the top stone was simply too heavy for two stones to bear. This time when I stepped through, I expected to be in a new place, but I had not anticipated that it would be in the middle of the night. Above me, countless stars shown, the heavens a rich panoply of sparkling lights. There was no sign of the day I had just left. I was in the presence of stars. "This," the voice said, "is the Gate of Stars. Here the forces of the cosmos flow into the earth where they meet the powers within the world, giving life for all beings." As it spoke, I remembered that the stars also gave direction, helping people find their way.

I felt myself in an awesome place. It was as if each star were a story seeking to be told, seeking to be known. I was overwhelmed. Although I felt no threat, I felt a little shaken and stepped back through the gate where I found myself to the north of the Howe on a late summer afternoon.

Now I was walking to the west where yet another standing stone awaited me. But before I could reach it, I passed by a mighty stone that lay fallen on the ground, its massive form split into three pieces. Overhead I heard the harsh cry of a crow. The voice said to me, "This is the Fallen Stone. It lost its way and could not stand. It lies as a warning. It could block the path if you are not careful."

I stepped carefully and went around it and on to the standing stone beyond which, frankly, did not appear in much better shape itself from the one on the ground, though it was still upright.

This stone was grey and old and was split at the top, the crack running almost its whole length, just stopping short of turning it into two stones side by side. As I approached it, a shiver went up my back, for it seemed foreboding to me. The voice said, "Fear not. This is the Stone of Release. Here you let go of whatever is not needed or has served its time and purpose."

I know this was meant to be reassuring, but I couldn't help but think, what if I am someone who has served my time? I hurried on to what I now knew was the westernmost portal.

Like the Gate of Stars, this one was also made of four stones, three upright and holding a fourth upon them. Again, I did not know if this had special significance or was merely a necessity because of the weight of the stone the other three carried. At their feet, a row of small standing stones seemed to mark a boundary. Gingerly, but feeling no resistance, I stepped over them and through the portal. I heard the voice saying, "This is the Gate of Twilight. This marks the threshold where one thing gives way to another and where the potential of the dawn is realized in the fulfillment of the evening."

Looking out to the west, I saw that in this new vista, the sun had already set. A bright star shone on the horizon above a range of mountains. I could see the river I had seen before flowing before me, but it seemed larger, more vast than I remembered. Was it in fact an inlet of the sea and were those lands and mountains I could see the fabled Western Isles of folklore and legend, the realm of the gods, the realm of those who have journeyed beyond the earth? If so, they were not the place for me. I stepped back gladly into the sunlight of the late afternoon.

Now there was only one stone left to see before I could complete the circle and presumably enter the Howe. I hurried towards it. Like the other standing stones in this outer circle, it too bore carvings upon its side. A smaller stone stood at its side. As I stood by it, I could see the strange river once again. The voice said, "This is the Stone of Return. The threshold once crossed is crossed again as the cycle returns to wholeness and is complete. Here endings and beginnings meet."

Feeling I had completed my own cycle of the stones, I hurried now towards the path into the Howe, sure that nothing further would bar my way. Curiosity burned within me to know what was in that ancient hill. But I was wrong. As I walked towards the Howe entrance, my eye caught movement near my feet. Looking down, I saw a huge snake curling around a stone that seemed to vibrate with power and energy. The serpent was moving towards me. My heart leapt in my chest, and I stopped, standing very still, hardly daring to breathe. The snake stopped its movement and lay still as well, seeming to wait for something. Was I in danger?

The faithful voice returned. "There is power in the earth! Can you befriend it? Can you make the world your ally? This is your chance. This is your choice!"

I wasn't sure what to do. The stone continued to radiate power, which seemed somehow to become part of the serpent that was coiled around it. None of us moved. And then, more out of instinct than anything, I reached forward gingerly but with increasing trust and acceptance and placed my hand upon the snake. I could feel the smooth scales and the powerful muscle beneath my fingers. And I could feel the energy rising from the earth. There was a flash....!

I found myself in a dark place, a strange, unearthly place, surrounded by stone walls that were obviously hewn by hand. I knew intuitively that I was within the Howe. In fact, before me was a stone raised up like an altar, and on it a candle burned. But that was all that was normal. In all other ways, it was a strange, unearthly place that seemed to connect with realms both within and beyond the earth. In one direction, I could see stars and the deep blackness of the cosmos, in another direction the sun burned brightly, and in a third the moon shone with a mysterious clear light. Stellar, Solar, Lunar and, with the stones about me, the Earthly: the four creative realms of ancient lore.

Though I seemed to have abandoned the familiar world, the familiar voice had not abandoned me. It now spoke to me, saying, "Fear not! You have accepted the power in the land. Now you stand at another portal. It is the fifth gate, the one that leads into the realm of the Sidhe, the people of peace and the guardians of the lands of Faerie. Do you wish to enter further? Once you enter, you must press forward."

I looked around at the stone and the visions of the celestial realms. This was what I had wanted. How could I not go further? "I will go on," I said aloud.

This time there was no flash of light, no transition. Instead, I found myself no longer in the stone chamber but standing in sunlight by the side of an ocean. Near me was an outcropping of stone and above it trees braved the elements to extend their branches out over the shore. By itself it was not an unusual scene. I had been to such places in my familiar world. But here I felt something different, as if the sky, sea, and land—and the plants upon the land—all were blended in a perfect harmony, each supporting the other, each part of the other. I felt a oneness that nonetheless honored the uniqueness of each individual form and life that it embraced.

Looking out over the ocean, I could see the far line of the horizon, and it seemed to me that something lay out there just beyond my sight, invisible yet somehow present with possibility. It was exciting. My heart felt at home in this place and yet yearned for what lay beyond.

"This is the vision that will guide you through your journey," said the ever-present voice. "This is a land of harmony, and beyond is the Far Country, the land of possibility. It is a land you can reach and create if you complete the journey, understand its lessons and accept the gifts it has to give you. Seeing this, feeling this, do you wish to proceed?"

"Yes," I said.

"Then remember the Vision."

The scene changed once again. Instead of being on the seashore with life all around me, I now found myself in a barren, rocky land filled with jagged cliffs and ridges. I stood on the edge of such a cliff, looking down at an abyss. The land beyond was hazy, hard to discern, but I thought I could see a river far below me and wondered for a moment if it were the river I had seen by the stones and portal to the west of the Howe. And I could see something else: a cave, and within it, stars. Overhead an eagle flew. Where was I now?

"You are on the Edge," said the voice. "Before you can enter the new, you must step beyond what is familiar. You must take courage and step into the unknown. Only then can you proceed."

"You mean, step into the abyss?" I was aghast.

"It's only an abyss from where you stand. Perhaps it is simply a step into new possibilities. Do you doubt you can do it? Summon your courage! Summon your trust in yourself!"

It was still a fearful step, but with this encouragement, I did as the voice suggested and summoned my courage. I closed my eyes and stepped off the edge.

I did not fall. In fact, I thought perhaps I had been further from the cliff edge than I'd thought and had merely taken a step towards the edge. I opened my eyes. To my astonishment, I was standing in a green and pleasant land. Before me was another standing stone, but one quite unlike anything I had ever seen before. Two thirds of it was in the rough shape of a bird, its breast and wings faintly discernible. But the head was that of a raptor whose black eyes now gazed fiercely upon me. So fine and delicate was the carving that I could see individual feathers. It seemed as if a giant living falcon were emerging from the stone. I marveled at the craft and skill of the artist who had created it.

Then the creature blinked at me.

Startled, I jumped back, my heart beating in my chest. The stone falcon blinked once more, and then it spoke, the familiar voice that had accompanied me on my journey speaking to me through its curved beak. "Your courage has given you wings," it said. "You saw the vision and you had faith. You have passed the test of flight. Your emergence is beginning."

With that, the stone fell away, and the falcon flew off into the sky.

Turning to watch it go, I saw not far behind me a magnificent building rising into the sky, a Sandhill Crane flying nearby. I had never seen such a structure before, though it was vaguely reminiscent of mountain lamaseries I had seen in pictures of Tibet. It was the only building I could see anywhere. Here, I thought, must live the rulers of this land, and I determined to seek them out and meet them.

But I had only gone a few steps when my familiar companion, the Invisible Voice, made its presence known again. "You may not go there," it said, its tone brooking no argument. I stopped.

"Is it forbidden?" I asked. "Who lives there?"

"I do," the voice answered.

"You?" I exclaimed. "But I would meet you, see you! You have been my guide…"

"And so I shall remain though you see me not, but you have other places to go, other things to see, other tasks to perform."

"But what is this place? It is beautiful!"

"It is the Palace of the Sidhe, the People of Peace, the Lords of the lands of Faerie. What you need to know is that they bid you welcome. You are a guest in this land, and the Palace will watch over you. I will watch over you."

I did not know what else to say. My heart longed to see this Palace for myself. I was sure its inhabitants would be as wonderful and beautiful as it looked to be. But as if my unseen guide had read my mind, the voice said, "We are not your destination. You are."

"I…I don't understand."

"We are not here to take you out of your world. We are here to bring you into it new ways. Once this is done, then you will see us. Of that you should have no doubt."

His words made little sense to me. They had brought me here through the Howe only to take me back to where I came from? It made little sense. But I felt I had no choice but to accept.

"Turn, my guest. Turn around and walk. In a short while, you will come to a well of living water, a pond fed by springs deep within the earth. Drink from it and you will find your further path revealed."

"Can you say more?" I asked. But there was only silence. So I reluctantly turned away from the beauty and splendor of the Palace and all the mystery and wonder that it promised, and began to walk into the gently rolling land ahead of me.

As the voice had promised, it was but a little while and a pleasant walk before I came to a spring where water indeed gushed forth from the earth, flowing into a circular pond like a deep well. I walked up to it and realized I was not alone. On the other side, a magnificent stag stood watching me calmly. It seemed perfectly unafraid at my approach. I wondered if in this land of Faerie it had ever seen a human being before. And then I wondered if indeed it was a stag or if it was itself a Faerie being.

My guide—was he indeed a Faerie Lord, I wondered—had said for me to drink, so I knelt by the well to do so. As I did, the stag came around the pool and lowered his head to the water next to me. I felt graced to be in the presence of such a creature. It seemed a special blessing. Putting my head down, I also drank from the pool. The water was cool and delicious. I felt filled with a vitality such as I had rarely experienced before.

Looking up, I saw the stag was gone. But then I saw it walking toward a distant row of trees.

It stopped and looked back at me over its shoulder, and I had the impression that it wanted me to follow. So I got to my feet and hastened after it.

When we reached the trees, the stag plunged into them, so I had no choice but to follow. Yet it was not arduous going. There was a path, and it was as if the trees themselves bent back to give us room to walk through their midst. I realized this was no mighty forest but only a narrow stand of trees, for soon we came to the end of them. The trees at the edge of the forest were flowering, beautiful white blossoms hanging from their branches. As the stag approached them, it began to disappear. Like a ghost, it grew more and more transparent until finally it vanished altogether.

I hurried forward to the place where it had been, flowers hanging from the branches above me. In front of me at my feet were green stalks of wheat growing at the edge of the trees. And beyond... beyond I saw fields bursting with grain, the fertility and abundance of the land displaying itself before me.

I stood for a moment in the shade of the trees, white blossoms swaying against my forehead in a light breeze, admiring the sight before me. I have always appreciated farmlands, and this was a delight for my eyes.

"You have beautiful lands," I said out loud, confident that my unseen guide would hear me.

"Thank you," came the reply as I was sure it would. "We bless our land, so we are blessed by it in return. But you must be hungry. Look to your right."

I turned and looked. There was a table set in the shade of the flowering trees. And on the table was a feast, the products of the land. There were cheeses and bread, apples and grapes and other fruits.

"Please," said the voice. "Eat and drink. Enjoy yourself with the gifts of the land."

I hesitated. I had heard tales told in the evening around fire-filled hearths of the dangers of accepting food in the Faerie lands. "If you eat Faerie food," one elder had said, nodding his head knowingly, "ye'll never come back. You will be their slave forever." I was sure this would not happen, and yet....

As if reading my mind, which by now I was sure was all too likely and possible for my unseen guide, the voice urged me to partake. "There is no danger here to you," it said, "only nourishment to give you strength. As I said, our desire is not to keep you here out of your world but to return you to it..."

"...changed," I said, interrupting.

The voice was still. Then it said, "yes, but only if you choose. We cannot force this change upon you." This gave me pause, but on the whole, I was reassured. So I fell to the feast with only the slightest trepidation. Soon even that was gone as the flavor and texture of the food drove all thoughts from my mind but the pleasure of the moment. As I ate, I was sure I saw eyes watching me from the shadows under the leaves, and small, greenish faces seemed to stare just at the edge of my vision. But nothing made any move towards me, and I thought, let them watch, whoever or whatever they are, and see the pleasure their food is giving me.

In time I became sated. As I finished, the voice returned and said, "I have only one request. That you drink both the wines, the red and the white." And suddenly there were two wine glasses on the table, one filled with a red liquid, one with a white. Perhaps I should have been concerned. But I had eaten well in the shade of flowering trees in a peaceful and abundant land. I was filled with contentment, and the wine seemed only a further part of that. I reached out and took the red wine glass in my hand and drained its contents. Then I did the same with the white. They were both exquisite, unlike any wines I had ever known before.

"Excellent!" I said. "Either one would have been sufficient. Both were...beyond words..."

"I am glad. The red wine was for you, the white wine was for us. They are the blood of your land and the blood of ours. Drinking them is our covenant with you...."

And with that the voice faded away, and I slept.

In sleeping, I saw a strange thing. Before me rose a mighty tree, one so tall I could not see the top of it. On one side of it, it was night, and I could see moon and stars in the sky. On the other side it was bright day lit by the sun. And I knew somehow without being told that the moonlit side was the realm of Faerie and the sunlit side was the land of humankind. In some magical way, the tree was a portal between the two, a threshold, perhaps even the World Tree of ancient myth and lore.

As I looked down, on the moonlit side I could see a pile of treasure—gold and jewels—piled up against the trunk of the tree. It was more wealth than I had ever seen in my life. My heart skipped and my pulse raced with the wanting of it. I made a step towards it. But then in the middle of the tree, I saw a space that was neither of one land nor the other, and in it there were piles of gold and piles of leaves and twigs. I looked further, and on the sunlit side there were only leaves. I knew then that the gold I coveted was Faerie gold, an illusion that was not what it seemed. Beautiful by night and under the glamour of Faerie, it appeared as fabulous wealth. But in the world of men and women, in the light of day, it would turn into its true nature, nothing but leaves and twigs, worthless.

I started to turn away, sure that this was some kind of test of discernment and that I had passed it by refusing the gold. But something, some instinct, stopped me. Perhaps this was a deeper test than it appeared. What if the illusion worked the other way as well, that something we humans saw as worthless was actually a treasure in the eyes of the Sidhe?

But what was valuable about leaves and twigs? Nothing. . . .
Unless you saw them through nature's eyes. Then they were
food for the soil. Gold and jewels had no nourishment but leaves and
twigs could decay. They provided sustenance for insects and bacteria.
Their substance returned to the soil and became food for the trees that
had shed them. They were part of the cycle of life, part of what made
that cycle unbroken, part of the wholeness of nature.

It was then that the colorful leaves and bent twigs became
beautiful and valuable in my sight. No merchant would have
accepted them as payment for anything, but they could make compost,
gardener's gold, which the soil would accept gladly. And it was the
soil, not a merchant that had produced the bounty on which I had
so recently feasted. No amount of gold could have purchased what
I ate had the land and nature not given birth to it in the first place.
And if that were true in Faerie, it was equally true in the world from
which I'd come.

So there was value on both sides of the tree. Each world had
treasure for the other. There was no deception here, only a deeper
understanding and a reconciliation that united both worlds.

I reached down, and with laughter, I picked up both leaves
and gold and put both in my pocket. Would the gold turn to leaves
in my world? Would the leaves turn to gold in the Faerie world? I
had no idea, but the thought of it filled me with delight. There was
no reason I could not honor both.

Midsummer's Day, June 21

The tree faded out of sight, and I was standing on the bank of a narrow, shallow river. Across from me on the other bank but partway into the water was a large, brown bear. But I could see that like the raptor, this creature was half stone as well.

The bear turned its shaggy head in my direction. Once more the voice of my invisible host spoke through its lips. "Well done! You have passed the test of discernment. This gives you strength for what is ahead, not just physical strength but moral and spiritual strength as well. You are starting to understand just what our world is about, for we are the keepers of the world's treasures, treasures we would gladly share if humanity knew how to appreciate and value them."

The bear shook itself, and the stone fell away. It came over to me, and I felt no fear, only love. "Good," it whispered, as it rubbed its head against my head. "Very good." Then it disappeared.

And I did, too.

I found myself no longer on a river bank but standing beside a great standing stone instead. It was night time, and a brilliant full moon shone in the sky above. Had I been magically returned to my world?

At my feet was a path, and I began to follow. I realized immediately I was not back where I had started. There were more great stones standing in the earth, but they were not in a circle. And when I saw where the path led, I knew beyond doubt I was still in the land of the Sidhe.

Ahead of me the path turned into a spiral bordered with flowers. From it a wide wooden staircase wound gracefully up into the sky where it blended with the moonlight, fading into the stars. It was a staircase of great beauty, one that might have come from the Palace I had seen earlier.

This time I felt no trepidation as I walked up to the staircase and prepared to mount it. I knew not where it might lead, but by now I had learned to trust magical transformations. I knew I had nothing to fear and perhaps much to gain. I placed my foot on the first step and waited, half expecting my host's voice to come again. But there was nothing, so I began to climb the stairs. As they wound to the left, I could see the stars through them, and the banister and railing seemed more fashioned from moonbeams than from wood. Higher I went, placing my eyes on the moon, feeling the steps beneath my feet rather than seeing them, and when at one point I glanced down, I was indeed standing on air and moonlight and nothing else. I took another step. . . .

. . . and found myself on a grassy plain in the midst of a sunny day. In front of me was a pile of books and scrolls as well as writing implements. One book was open, propped up against the pile. And as I watched, starlight began to pour down in a stream from the sky above. It was a column of sparkles that resolved itself to my amazement into a red creature that seemed to be a Phoenix or even a small dragon. It looked at me and when it spoke, I heard my invisible host's voice one more.

"Three gifts we give you. The first you have already experienced, or you would not be here. This is the ability to walk between the worlds, to mount the stairs of discernment and inner attunement to find new worlds of consciousness and spirit. The second gift is that of the wisdom and knowledge that you can gain when you open your heart and mind to the world and its multiple dimensions. This is symbolized by these books and scrolls before you."

"And the third gift?" I asked when the voice paused.

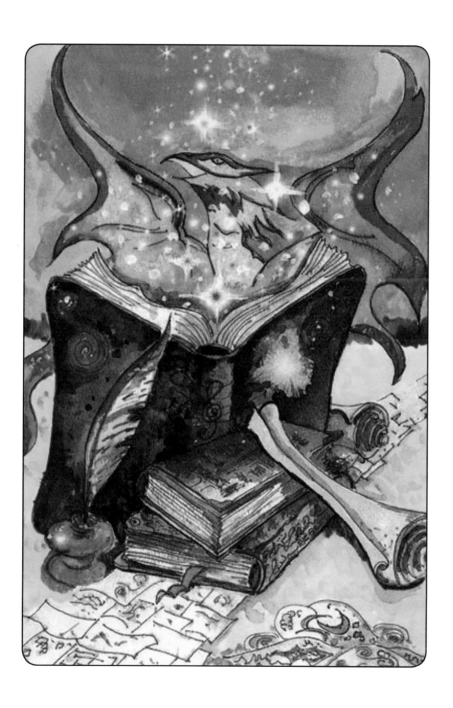

"The third is the gift of Faerie Luck."

The dragon-phoenix waved its wings, and I suddenly saw a coin flipping in the air. "Call it!" said the voice.

"Heads," I said, without thinking, and the coin landed in the midst of flowers where butterflies were hovering or drinking nectar. I looked at it. On its side was engraved a golden four-leaf clover.

"Heads it is!" said the voice.

I picked up the coin and looked at it. On the other side it was blank.

"Toss it again," my host said. I did, and as it flew through the air, I said, "Heads again!" And once more it landed with the clover showing.

"So," I said, picking up the coin once more, "the third gift is a lucky coin?"

The voice chuckled and I could have sworn the little dragon creature smiled. "Oh, it's much more than that! One who is a partner to the world, blended with it in love and respect, gains a relationship that can influence the probability of outcomes. Such a person knows the interconnections of all things. That understanding, which is native to my people the Sidhe, gives an attunement to the world that allows us to affect how things unfold. We know how the smallest influence, like the fluttering of the wings of those butterflies, can create the largest effect. This gives us a way to manifest, to heal and to bless. It is this ability the coin represents, and it is our third gift to you." Having said this, the dragon-phoenix flapped its wings once more and disappeared, along with the books and scrolls.

I felt an urge to walk. The day was pleasant and warm, and the meadow about me was inviting with its flowers and various colored butterflies seeking after nectar. I picked a direction and set off. Surprisingly, my unseen host continued his discourse as if he were still at my side. In a way I suppose he was, though I pictured him, whatever he looked like, sitting comfortably and at ease in a grand room in the Palace while my legs were the ones getting a workout. Still, in such a pretty countryside, I was pleased to be doing so.

"You remember," he said, "the vision you had of the Far Country, the possible country, at the beginning of your journey? The one that led you to the edge?"

"Yes."

"That is the world we desire to see come about, a world of wholeness and new possibilities. And it can when our race and yours are reconciled and once again united. Once we were one people, both filled with life and energy from the stars, but then we divided. You became part of the earth. And we retreated into a magical realm of our own. Now it is time to come together again for the sake of the future."

We came to a low stone wall. Looking down I saw growing out of the cracks in the rock a red rose and a white rose entwined. Next to them was an ancient stone goblet or chalice.

"We grow from the same soil," my host said. "Your blood is red, mine is white, but we are the same spirit. Red wine and white, white rose and red, we have different gifts and qualities, but now is the time to blend them in a grail of compassion and wholeness for the world. Now is the time for a new being to emerge who carries the spirit of us both."

On impulse, I knelt and picked up the ancient chalice, a grail cup, and drank from the liquid it held. It was not wine, nor was it water, nor like anything else I had ever tasted, but it filled a place in me I had not known was empty and quenched a thirst I had only dimly realized I had. I could feel something shifting deep within me, a new consciousness stirring and expanding the familiar boundaries that had defined my "normal" life.

I put the stone grail back by the wall and stood. Silence was all about me. I knew somehow my unseen host had left. To my right I could see a small passage leading through the stone wall, and I knew that was where I must go. But when I walked through it and into the other side, the world changed once again. From daylight I now entered into night. Stars twinkled in the sky. A full moon, like the one into whose light the magical stairs had taken me, shone in their midst. In this place, time and space obviously were matters of convenience, not of law.

Another light caught my attention. Off to my left, a small campfire burned. I could see a figure sitting cross-legged in front of it, reminding me of a picture I had once seen of an old shaman. I could hear a curious tapping sound, like metal hitting stone. I went over, and as I got nearer, I could see that it was a man naked from the waist up, and he had a hammer and chisel in his hands with which he was chipping at stone in his lap. But closer still, I saw to my astonishment that he was, like the falcon and the bear before him, partly encased in stone. It was this stone that he was chipping, bringing forth his legs.

"Sit down," he said, not surprisingly in the voice of my host. He kept chipping away as he spoke. I did as he asked. "A new humanity is emerging from the earth," he said. Chip, chip, chip went the chisel against his thigh. "Now you do this by your own efforts. No one but you can decide to free yourself from the encasements you have created." Chip, chip, chip. "But we can help. All the earth can help, if you will see the world and the creatures within it as your allies and your partners." He paused from his chipping. "When you do, you will not need to chip this stone alone."

At that moment, the stone around him fell away, and he stood, free and powerful before me. He gestured towards the fire. He may have thrown something on it, for suddenly it flared up, momentarily blinding me. And as I might have expected, when I could see again, the stone shaman was not there.

Instead, I was in a cavern, one filled with a strange luminescence that seemed to come from all the walls so that I had no trouble seeing. In front of me was a small pool in which I could see fish darting about. Beyond, carved from stone, was a graceful and beautiful throne. A small fire burned before it. By its side lay a wolf whose black eyes stared at me in challenge and expectation, and on its back perched an owl. Next to it rested another grail. Even a spider was present.

One more a voice spoke, but this time it was a woman's voice, one that thrilled my heart to hear and awoke ancient memories in the very cells of my body. "Welcome," she said, "to the Throne of Gaia. It is the Throne of the Four-Fold Alliance, the partnership of humanity, creatures, Faerie, and Gaia. It is the Throne that restores an ancient oneness in the name of a present that needs healing and a future that needs birthing. Whoever sits here must hold love and the wholeness of all in his or her heart. Not all will choose to sit here, but whoever does will gain the spirit of Gaia within them and be servant, friend, and partner to all. Will you sit?"

"Gladly," I said. And putting action to my intent, I stepped around the pool and the fire and sat upon this ancient throne. A rush of joy filled my heart, and I felt as if all the earth were my Self.

And then, once more, I was elsewhere.

I stood once more in the outer ring of the stone circle where my journey had begun. Next to me was the dark, shadowed form of the Reaper stone, and I knew indeed that a part of me had died and a new me had been born. Across the water, I could see the land that awaited, a new land, a new world. I felt a pang of sadness, for it seemed far from me, and it was where I wanted to be with all my strength and soul.

As I reached towards it in longing, a robin flew down and landed on my finger, raising its voice in joyous song. I held my breath. Then I knew. Here was the new land! Here was the Four-Fold Alliance made flesh: bird, standing stone and me: creature, Sidhe, and human, all within the world at large, the body and spirit of Gaia. It was within me if I opened to it. It was all around me if I would but see it. Gaia was everywhere I was, and I could be a partner wherever I might be. The Throne was not in some deep magical cavern but in the depths of my life, in love shared with others, and in the magic of a shared world awakening.

The little robin sang even more joyously, and in that moment, that distant land did not seem far away at all.

Create Your Own Magical Journeys

If you enjoyed this journey and would like to explore your own relationship with the Sidhe, then you can go back and use the images to create your own magical journey. Ignore the story as it is written and just attune to the images, seeing what narrative emerges for you. What does each picture mean to you? What does it invoke? For example, the story begins with the Ancestor Stone. This represents your starting place, where you are now and the roots and causes in your past that have brought you to this moment in time and circumstance. What are those "ancestors" or causes for you? Where are you in your life right now? What possibilities do you feel could unfold from where you are now or from the "ancestors" within you?

Each picture can offer its own special insights to you when you frame it within the context of your own life. Just ask what it means to you right now as you look at it and see what emerges. Or simply allow your own narrative interpretations to unfold as you go through the book.

Of course, the pictures in this book offer only one possible sequence. If you would like more versatility or would like to go deeper into the experience these images can offer, perhaps you would be interested in the card deck from which this book is derived. Owning the cards themselves would allow you to arrange them in any sequence you wish or allow a narrative sequence to emerge randomly. This can be a powerful way to gain insights into your own life and journey. If you are interested, the *Card Deck of the Sidhe* and Manual are available through the Lorian Association website bookstore at www.lorian.org. This 33 card premium deck and instruction manual offers a full complement of additional meditations, journeys, layouts and oracular uses of the images in this book.

Blessings to all who encounter the People of Peace,

David Spangler

Midsummer's Day, June 21

The Story of
A Midsummer's Journey with the Sidhe

And here is the remarkable story behind the development of the Card deck and the subsequent journey you have just completed.

The story of how *The Card Deck of the Sidhe* came into being is a true fairy story. (Actually, to use the proper spelling for the beings involved, it is a Faery story, but I'll have more to say on that later.) The story begins when my Lorian colleague Jeremy Berg, the owner and publisher of Lorian Press, published *The Sidhe*, a book by the British spiritual teacher and author, John Matthews. *Sidhe* (pronounced shee) is, according to John, the "oldest known name for the faery races of Ireland" and means the "people of peace."

This book became very popular and eventually led to a demand for more material about the Sidhe. Unfortunately, although he would have liked to do so, John Matthews was too busy to write a sequel. Knowing my love of designing card decks (I had already designed two for him, the *Manifestation Card Deck* and *The Soul's Oracle*), Jeremy asked if I'd like to create a card deck about the Sidhe. I was intrigued, but unlike John or R.J. Stewart or Orion Foxwood, two other friends and authors who have written several books about the Sidhe, I knew very little about these beings. While I have had extensive contact with the invisible, subtle worlds of spirit and those who dwell upon them, I had had virtually no communication with the Sidhe or indeed with any Faery being that I knew of. So I told Jeremy that I didn't feel I was capable of such a task.

That is where things were left for several months. But then, in the winter of 2011, something unexpected happened that changed everything. Taking a break from writing, I was sitting on the sofa in my living room and just staring out the window at the trees and bushes beyond when I felt a presence in the room behind me. Turning around, I saw in my mind's eye a swirling, shifting, radiant mist in the air near the fire place. At the same time I felt another mind in touch with my own and heard it say, "I am one of the Sidhe, and I've come to help you with the card deck." This being no sooner said this than there flashed into my mind a complete picture of what a Sidhe card deck would look like when laid out and the major components of what such a deck should contain. There were few details—they came later—but the basic pattern was very clear.

The book that you're holding is one part of the result of the collaboration that started with that meeting.

The initial contact was very brief, lasting no more than five minutes, but it was long enough and comprehensive enough that I knew beyond any doubt that I could create a card deck of the Sidhe. I knew now what was needed and how to go about it. With this new-found confidence, I phoned up Jeremy, explained what had happened and asked if he was still interested in publishing a Sidhe deck. He certainly was, and so the project began.

In the previous card decks I had done, Jeremy's daughter Deva Berg had been the artist, and she had been truly inspired. But she was now a new mother and was too busy to undertake another project. So Jeremy himself decided to paint all the cards. In the process, a remarkable three-way partnership unfolded between Jeremy and I and the Sidhe.

There were some initial guidelines. For instance, we were asked not to portray the Sidhe themselves in the cards; no images or pictures of them were allowed in order to prevent imposing a particular form either upon the Sidhe themselves or upon the imagination of a person using the cards. There could be no more than thirty-three cards, and I have no idea why that particular number was a limit. Obviously this deck was not to be anything like a traditional Tarot which has seventy-eight cards.

Half of the cards were to be of standing stones arranged in a circle around a central Howe or hill with portals at each of the four directions; these cards represented a fixed element within the deck. The other half were the fluid element, forming a ring of moving qualities as if faeries were dancing around the stone circle. The stones were of the earth, the outer ring, called "Dancers," was of the invisible world of the Sidhe.

From the standpoint of the Sidhe who contacted me, the overall purpose of the card deck was to act as a point of potential contact between a user and the energetic realm of the Sidhe. This contact would take place within the imagination and the subtle energy fields of the user and would be unique to each person. This was one reason the Sidhe wished there to be no images of them that might force a user to think of them in ways that someone else did. It was evident that my faerie contact wished each person to come to the deck and to use it with fresh and unconditioned imagination and expectation.

By the same token, I felt that there needed to be an oracular use to the deck, a way to tap not only the imagination but the intuition of the individual and the subtle energy field of possibilities and potentials within a situation. I felt the deck should be useful to the individual beyond being a meditation tool, important as that function might be. I wished it also to be a tool that a person might use to gain deeper insights into life issues that they might be confronting. I hoped the deck would not only facilitate contact and a felt sense of connection with the Sidhe themselves and the state of consciousness they represent; I hoped it would also enable a person to tap into that state of consciousness to find insights and help in engaging creatively and holistically with the world around them.

All these considerations went into creating the pictures that make up this deck. Painting the standing stones was relatively simple. There were eight of them and four portals or gates; Jeremy used pictures of actual standing stones as models for the cards he painted. When I first saw them, I was struck with the power that the images conveyed.

It was with the sixteen "dancers" that the fun really began. I had no idea when we started just what these cards would be, only that in some manner they would represent qualities, states of being, or images useful both in attuning to the Sidhe and in contributing to an oracular function. A tall order! It was in this area that the collaboration most manifested itself.

I began by making lists, jotting down all the card ideas I could think of that might be appropriate. As I did so, specific ideas and images began to come from our Sidhe partner. Certain of my choices were eliminated quickly and others were considered or counter-suggestions were made. As the final list began to take shape, I would pass on my ideas to Jeremy and he would turn them into a painted picture. At the same time, Jeremy began to feel his own contact with the Faerie world and would receive specific images, sometimes quite different from the ones I had suggested. For a time, both he and I would awaken around 4 am in the morning, he with specific images in his mind and me with ideas and patterns. Then at a more reasonable hour we would compare notes over the phone and discover that we were both thinking of the exact same ideas and images. Obviously, our Sidhe partner was communicating with both us in the dream state and we were both receiving suggestions—often the same suggestion—from this being who was taking a very involved and "hands on" approach to the creation of this card deck.

In this way, the sixteen "Dancer" cards evolved into the forms you have now in this Sidhe card deck. As they did so, I was delighted to discover that far from being random, each card was a part of an unfolding story. It is the story of a journey into the realm of the Sidhe, undergoing a transformative initiation and returning to the outer world. This story forms the basis of this book.

The end result of this collaboration is what I believe to be a very powerful tool for both attunement to a related species of intelligence that shares this world with us and is concerned about earth's future and use as an oracular portal into your own intuition. The manner in which it emerged is a testament to what is possible when collaboration and partnership with inner beings is accepted and engaged. Although Jeremy and I certainly added our human perspectives and insights to its creation, I have no doubt that this deck of cards is a gift of love and an invitation from the Sidhe. It is truly a faery story come to life. I hope you will find it a source of blessing.

David Spangler

Further Reading List

Red Tree, White Tree, by Wendy Berg

Meeting Fairies: My Remarkable Encounter with Nature Spirits, by R. Ogilvie Crombie (sold in England under the title, *The Gentleman and the Faun*)

Working With Angels, Fairies, and Nature Spirits, by William Bloom

The Romance of the Faery Melusine, by Gareth Knight

The Tree of Enchantment, by Orion Foxwood

Memoirs of an Ordinary Mystic, by Dorothy Maclean

How to See Faeries, by John Matthews and Brian Froud

The Sidhe, by John Matthews

Card Deck of the Sidhe, by David Spangler

Subtle Worlds: An Explorer's Field Guide by David Spangler

The Living World of Faery by R. J. Stewart

The Well of Light by R. J. Stewart

If you would like to purchase the **Card deck of the Sidhe** you can do so through the Lorian Bookstore at www.lorian.org. It is composed of 33 full color, premium 3.5" X 5" cards in a fabric carrying pouch and a manual outlining meditative and oracular uses of the cards. It comes packaged in a sturdy box with a clear lid and full color box sleeve.

Mention in your Lorian order that you own this book and you automatically qualify for a 10% discount off the $33.00 cover price.

A Midsummer's Journey with the Sidhe

Book Design, Illustrations and Cover Art
Copyright © 2011 Jeremy Berg

Published by Lorian Press
2204 E Grand Ave.
Everett, WA 98201

10 Digit ISBN: 0-936878-38-X
13 Digit ISBN: 978-0-936878-38-6

Spangler/David
A Midsummer's Journey with the Sidhe/David Spangler

First Edition July 2011

Printed in the United States of America

0 9 8 7 6 5 4 3 2 1

www.lorian.org

CPSIA information can be obtained
at www.ICGtesting.com
Printed in the USA
LVIC04n0556200215
427376LV00007B/2